Wisdom, Magic and Miracles

Tools for today; Wisdom for life

Wisdom, Magic and Miracles
Tools for today; Wisdom for life

Published by JingotheCat.com
Book designed by Andy Grachuk

Forward

Thank you for buying "Wisdom, Magic, and Miracles". This book is a culmination of wisdomatic sayings I have heard and read since I awakened in 2003. From these wisdomatic sayings I have created my own interpretations. These tools for today will be wisdom for life.

These wisdomatic sayings have changed my life from diagnosed severe depression and anxiety disorders to calmness, peace of mind, and happiness. I know these will help you too.

Ask a friend or family member to go on this journey with you. Once you start practicing these sayings together, you will be able to be each other's spiritual advisors.

Keep it in the moment.
Stu

Acknowledgements

I would like to make the following personal acknowledgements for the making of this book, "Wisdom, Magic, and Miracles."

Thanks to all the people, teachers, and experiences from which I have gathered this collection of wisdom, magic, and miracles from. I will be forever grateful.

Thanks to my beautiful wife Angela for her inspiration, patience, and computer skills.

Thanks to Eric and Jackie Aquilio and Colt of Sign Language Signs for the magic of the cover art.

Thanks to Alexandra "Lil A" Foran for shining her light on The Organic Angel and for her editing skills.

Final acknowledgement goes out to Andy Grachuk from Jingothecat.com for making this book come to fruition.

" The harder it is to love someone, the more love they need."

When you meet people who are not friendly, it means that they have had a pretty tough life. It is very easy to sink to their level and be angry with them, and have it ruin your day. Instead, kill them with kindness and watch what happens. I think you will be surprised.

"Don't put a question mark where God puts a period."

Sometimes in life we keep forcing something to happen and it doesn't, and we don't understand why.

Why not try surrendering and talking to a spiritual counselor or a good friend?

Sometimes it is God tapping you on the shoulder wanting you to take a different path.

"If you want to get to know God better,
get to know God's Children."

One of the mysteries of life is God. When we ask God for help, God sends people. So, certainly if we want to get to know God better, we must get to know God's children better, and treat them as we want to be treated.

"God, grant me the serenity to accept the things I cannot change, the courage to change the things I can and the wisdom to know the difference."

All people want peace and serenity. If we say this prayer and practice it, it shall be so.

We need to accept the fact that we can't change people, places, or things. The only thing we can change is ourselves. When we finally figure this out, peace and serenity can enter into our lives.

" Thank you God for all the things you have given me and all the things you have taken away."

*E*verything happens for a reason. Sometimes we find out why and sometimes we don't.

Instead of wasting the day being depressed over yesterday's losses, find gratitude for them and stay focused on the gratitude for the things you have today.

"True humility is not thinking less of yourself
it is thinking of yourself less."

Humility is one of the most misunderstood words.
Most people think it's associated with humiliation,
well it is not. It means to be humble which is the opposite of
ego and selfishness.

It's hard to pray to God if you think that you are God
yourself, and it's even harder to be an egomaniac with an
inferiority complex. Less self, less problems.

"Fear knocked, Faith answered."

ost humans have unpleasant reactions to life, such as anger, ego, hatred, judgment, and dishonesty, which are all fear based emotions.

When we become aware and are able to put a name to the emotion that we have been feeling all of our life, then we get an opportunity to change, and not let fear call the shots in our life.

The answer is to trust and believe in God and walk through our fears.

The magic and miracles wait for you on the other side.

"Doing the same thing, expecting different results is the true meaning of insanity."

Most people are creatures of habit. Even if we know that something we are doing is not good for us, we still continue doing it.

Break the cycle today, dare to kick one of your bad habits. Ask a friend for help, or join a support group.

When we become aware of the vicious cycle of addiction, and dare to change it, that's when the miracles start to happen.

"Expectation is premeditated resentment."

How many times have you expected something from somebody and they continue to fall short of your expectation? Then you become angry and start thinking unpleasant thoughts about that person.

Instead try thinking high hopes with no expectations. If you have no expectations you will have a lot more peace in your life. Then, if someone gives you something it will be a pleasant surprise.

"Living to learn and learning to live."

*D*id you ever wonder why God gave us two ears and one mouth?

It is more important to listen, than talk when learning new things.

Check in with yourself and see if you are the person who is talking all the time or are saying nothing at all.

Remember, conversation should be a two way street. Sometimes talking, sometimes listening. Sometimes student, sometimes teacher.

"Don't go to your personal darkroom,
where you develop your negatives."

A lot of people isolate and spend time alone because of fear caused by being hurt so many times.

Spending time alone thinking negatively will only make your depression worse.

Instead, make a change and get out and find positive people doing positive things.

If you don't think this will work for you, your misery will be happily refunded.

"You are only as sick as your secrets."

Most people hold on to their secrets because they think that they are the only ones who have suffered abuse or caused abuse.

The truth is that the world is filled with both types of people. The only ones that are not in their own self-made prisons with their fear, guilt, and shame are the ones who have shared their secrets with a trusted friend or spiritual advisor. You are not the only one.

"Going back in history causes depression, going to the future causes anxiety, try to live where your feet are, in the moment, where God lives."

We have all heard the word Zen. It means living in the present moment. To find peace, serenity, and happiness, we must become aware of our thoughts. Check in with yourself and think about what you are thinking about. If you are in history, bring it back to the moment. If you are in the future, bring it back to the moment. Happiness is found in the moment where God lives.

"Today is a gift that's why it's called the present."

Many people waste moments and days dwelling in negativity. They are complaining and thinking about what they don't have. Instead, stay focused on gratitude on what you have today. Don't neglect to tell loved ones that you love them, and don't take anyone or anything for granted.

Here today, gone tomorrow. Don't waste a day. All moments are precious. We have all come to this planet to awaken and to learn our lessons before it is too late.

"Ignorance, prejudice, and fear walk hand and hand."

A natural reaction to the unknown, such as different types of people and cultures, can create fear.

We are all the same on the inside. The truth is, if we hate others, we hate ourselves.

Instead of fear calling the shots and hating what we don't know, take time to learn about other people, places, and things. If you decide you still don't like them, try killing them with kindness. To truly become a spiritual warrior, we must become colorblind.

"Work smart, not hard."

*I*t has been said that all things are hard until they become easy.

Only through practice, understanding, and patience, can we figure out the best way to achieve a goal.

Using this mindset as we work our way through each day we can then put into practice thinking in each conscious moment if there is an easier way to do this particular project. One way to determine this is if we have peace of mind. Then we can be sure we are working smart, not hard.

"What you do to the earth, you do to yourself."

The earth that we live on is the reason why we are all able to sustain life on this planet.

If we disrespect ourselves, we are most likely going to disrespect others and mother nature.

Think twice before flicking your cigarette into nature, or throwing trash onto the ground. Be sure to incorporate recycling into your daily life.

"Only those who aren't afraid to die can then truly live."

A lot of people are afraid to die because of fear of the unknown. Letting fear rule the day and not letting your spirit roam free is a waste of your day.

Walk through your fears and let your childlike wonder take over.

Before you know it, you'll be living the life you have always dreamed of.

"Only those who aren't afraid to get their heart broken can then find true love."

All people have been hurt in one way or another. The normal reaction is to protect against getting hurt again. The only problem is you end up in your own self-made prison.

The key to life is to dare to open yourself up to love and life, and God will find the right person for you on God's time, not yours.

"Coincidence is God's way of staying anonymous."

When you run around crazy and your mind is everywhere except in the moment, you miss out on the God stories.

When you awaken to the day and the moment you will start to notice a lot of coincidences.

This is God's way of smiling down upon you. We are here on the planet to awaken to the magic of the moment where God lives.

"Life is a mystery to be solved,
not a problem to be solved."

*I*f you talk to most people, they will tell you all the problems that they have.

We all have a choice: positive or negative. The easier path is to speak negatively, the more difficult path is to speak positively. For instance, what is right with your day and what are you grateful for today? When we turn negatives into positives we will be pleasantly surprised on how our world changes.

"If you go around pointing a finger at other people because of your problems, remember that you have three fingers pointing back at yourself."

Most people love to blame everyone else for their problems. People point fingers at everyone else and never see the part they play or accept blame for anything they have done.

When we dare to look within and see what we have done, we can then learn from our mistakes and try not to make them again. Remember, we can only change ourselves, we cannot change other people.

"When we are caught in an emotion,
we can't heal ourselves."

One thing we need to learn is to ask people for help, especially when we are emotionally unbalanced. Asking people for help, doesn't mean we are weak, it means we are smart. We need to talk to a person we can trust. If we react to a situation, caught in the emotion, we will be in the wrong every time. We need to share the problem and find the best way of resolving it with the help of another person who is not caught in the emotion. Don't go it alone.

"Anxiety is fear out of control."

When we don't live in the present, and we are thinking of the future, this can cause anxiety and fear. We can't predict the future. When our minds go into the future and start playing mental movies of worst case scenarios, this causes fear and anxiety.

To cure this problem, we must have some kind of faith to believe in, that whatever is to be will be. We must stay grounded and present in the moment with positivity and gratitude. Fear is lack of faith. All is okay in this moment.

"When it's the hardest to have faith and hope, that's when you need it the most."

*P*racticing faith and hope on a regular basis is a full time job, and is quite a task to take on.

When life throws us a curve ball we start to question all that we know is good and true.

This is the time we need help from our friends and spiritual advisors to let us know that we are okay and to make sure that we are on the right track.

Life is sometimes like boot camp. These are tests and life lessons designed to help us grow. It's your choice.

"Don't sweat the small stuff, and it's all small stuff."

When we are caught in an emotion that doesn't feel good, we end up blowing it out of proportion because we make it all about us. When "I" becomes the main focus it becomes ego.

Instead, become aware of all the things in your life to be grateful for. Make your full time job turning negatives into positives.

One thing that happens to people all too often is that they don't realize what they had until they lost it. Don't wait until it is too late to make an amends to an old friend or tell the people around you how important they are to you.

"When you plot revenge, plan on digging two graves, one for them and one for yourself."

When someone does something bad to you, most people's reaction is to think of how to get back at them or plot their revenge.

When we do this we are sinking to their level and creating ego versus ego.

What we do to others, we do to ourselves. Instead, have compassion for these people for they are sick and suffering. Remember, hurt people, hurt people. Kill them with kindness. They are only repeating what was done to them. Stop the cycle today. You will be the one who comes out smiling.

"The three A's for living are Awareness, Attitude, and Action."

When you awaken to life, there are three important tools to use along the way.

First, we must awaken to ourselves in the moment. This is the awareness. Then, we may choose to try to change ourselves, this is the attitude. Finally, we must take the action, for without action this is only theoretical.

Make these three A's a part of your life today and feel God smiling down upon you as you transform yourself into the person you know you can be.

"You can't satisfy unsatisfied people."

Are you constantly seeking the approval from people and never receiving it? Are you a people pleaser and never pleasing people?

This is because these people are unsatisfied with themselves. So there can be no satisfaction in their lives.

Instead of wasting energy on those people spend that time working on yourself.

People Pleasing is a powerful addiction, which will need a lot of professional help. Remember the three A's for life: Awareness, Attitude, and Action.

"You can't be in the moment with a positive attitude and be depressed at the same time."

Most humans suffer from depression from time to time or on a constant basis.

If this is the case, it is usually caused by living in the past or feeling like you don't have enough.

Practice gratitude and positivity in each moment of life. Try to find what's right with your life instead of what's wrong.

"It doesn't matter where we come from it's who we are today."

Some people drag their past around like bags of heavy luggage. Some have guilt and regrets of their past actions. Some wish that good times of the past could be here today and some continue to relive the traumas of the past into their present day.

This is where the three A's for living come into play. The most important thing is to become aware that we are doing this and change our attitude about it - that we don't want this in our day anymore.

Then take action and try to keep our mind in the moment with a positive attitude of gratitude, and when the darkness of the past tries to creep in, bring it back to the moment.

"When the pain of change is less than the pain that you are experiencing, that's when you will become willing to do something about it."

Everyone knows how difficult it is to change. Some older people say that they are too old to change. Change would cause a new discomfort that they are not familiar with. People just get used to the pain that they are in and are not willing to put effort into the change that would make their life better.

We must walk through the pain of change to reap the reward of freedom on the other side. We must go through the desert to get to the top of the mountain.

"When we ask God for help, God sends people."

One very good way to start the day is to ask God for help. It is also recommended to be grateful for the day in which God has written for us.

God works through people. When we ask God for help any time throughout the day, and practice the moment, we will start to see people coming into our lives just at the right time we need them.

This is God's way of staying anonymous, this is God's way of letting you know he is with you and smiling down upon you with unconditional love.

" Try to live life with no traumas, dramas, issues, and tissues."

ost people are addicted to traumas, dramas, issues, and tissues whether you like them or not, or whether you are aware of them or not.

There can be no peace of mind in this mode. We are not supposed to be in fight or flight mode all the time. This is what is causing most of the illness in humanity.

We need to slow down, stop drinking so much caffeine and alcohol, and start practicing single tasking. We need to reconnect with nature and start paying attention to things that are really important in our lives before it is too late.

Dare to change and be part of the solution and not part of the problem.

"Be a door prize, not a doormat."

Some people are born into being people pleasers, due to unfortunate circumstances in their family dynamics.

That was then and this is now. It is okay to help people but we need to check our motives.

If we are doing it so people will like us, we are doing it for the wrong reasons.

If someone asks us for help and we truly don't want to do it, it is okay to say, "No thank you." "No thank you," is a complete sentence. Be good to yourself today and stop the people pleasing cycle.

"Don't mistake kindness for weakness."

*S*ome people think that if you are nice you are an easy target to be steam rolled.

While it is important to be nice to people we must have boundaries. Letting people know when they have stepped on your toes is an important part of self-esteem. However that person takes it, is none of your business. Only accountable people will accept what you have said, apologize, and try not to do it again.

"Ego is who is right, Humility is what is right."

More often than not, ego is in the driver's seat in most people's lives. Ego calls the shots, whether we are right, wrong, or indifferent.

Instead of needing to be right all the time can't we open ourselves to the fact that we don't know everything, and whatever other people want to believe is okay too?

Humility is an important tool to use daily. It lets God know we are not in charge and we trust and believe that God is. If God is your copilot, change seats with him.

It's only through awareness that we can begin to live in harmony with man and nature.

"Some say 'I will believe it when I see it,' others say when I believe it that's when I will see it.'"

It can be hard to believe in something you can't see. However, most people believe in electricity which you can't see moving through the wires.

God works through people, just like electricity. You can always tell because that person will always be lit up like a light bulb.

Once we understand this, within each moment, we will see God working through us and the people around us. It is an unmistakable feeling when God is working through you to help his children.

"Most people don't have any problems,
only the ones going on between their ears."

The most common problems people face on a daily basis is the inability to stay grounded in the moment.

The truth is, if you check in with yourself right here, right now you are okay.

It's only when your mind wonders from the moment and starts projecting into the future that you begin to cause problems in your own life. This causes unnecessary fears resulting in anxiety.

The moment is the answer to all of the problems you think you have going on between your ears.

"If you want to get to know God, get to know his children. We must learn to love his children, the way God loves us. The harder it is to love God's children, the more love they need."

Once awakened, we need to ask God for help. God's help is available 24/7. When we ask God for help, God sends people. God works through people. This is why we must try to get to know God's children even if they annoy us.

We can't fathom the amount of love God has for us, so try to love his children as best as we know how.

The harder it is to love some of his children, the more love they need. Sometimes we have to do this from afar.

"Monkey see, Monkey do, Monkey get in trouble too."

We are all influenced by people, places, and things. Some are good, some are not so good, and some are bad.

Sometimes it feels good to do the wrong thing and we are willing to pay the price for it.

This is why we need help from a spiritual advisor, to be able to ask questions like, "is this good for me?"

The punishment is in the act so why not try doing the next right thing: trying to have a healthy mind, body, and spirit.

Why not try helping people less fortunate than you? There is no bad side effect for doing the next right thing.

"You have to go through a lot, to become a lot."

We all have to go through the desert, to get to the mountain top.

Life is a teacher and we must go through each challenge to gain the experience to find out what works and what doesn't.

Too often people say that they regret the past and they feel they have wasted time.

Nothing happens in God's world for no reason. If mistakes were made we need to learn and grow from them.

"Fear - identify it, and then rectify it."

ℛeacting to situations in your life is fear calling the shots. Become aware of yourself in the moment and notice when you react to different things in a negative way, such as anger, addiction, being mean, and prejudice.

Believe it or not, this is you being afraid. Fear must be identified, than we must ask God for help to relieve us of this paralyzing character defect.

When we warrior up and walk through our fears there is always magic waiting on the other side.

*"If I change the way I see the world,
the world I see changes."*

When you dislike yourself and the world you live in, the universe reflects this back at you.

Just for today, try liking yourself. You are not as bad as you think you are. Forgive yourself and others.

As Gandhi said, "Be the change you wish to see in the world." The world is a beautiful place, if you would only see it this way.

You have the choice today to be grateful and thankful. Become aware of all the things this world has to offer you then begin to see the magic and miracles.

"Even if you are on the right track, you will get run over if you just sit there."

Many people are on the right track. They are awakening to the moment and trying to change and live right by practicing healthy mind, body, and spirit.

Each day we must continue working out at the spiritual gym, working through any challenges the creator puts in front of us for growth. Remember, there is no growth in the comfort zone.

Each day set one new goal for yourself that you know will make a positive change in your life.

These changes will not feel good at first, which is why most people will not change. We must be patient to reap the rewards of change.

"When learning, it is better to listen than talk, that's why God gave us two ears and one mouth."

No matter what age you are, it is still important to learn. So when learning, it is more important to listen than to talk.

Also, we should be trying to live in balance. So when we are having a conversation it is important to be a good listener as well as a talker. Become aware of the conversationalist in you and make any changes necessary to find balance. Nobody wants to be known as the "chatty Cathy."

"Don't let the seed of resentment turn into a plant."

Resentment is a mind virus that runs rampant in most people's lives. It is caused by being treated unfairly.

Once again we must see how this virus is toxic in our lives. Become aware of it, squash it before it becomes a plant growing roots in our mind and trying to find a home for life.

The only way to uproot this weed is the act of forgiveness. Forgiving someone or something does not mean what was done is okay. It just means we are aware that someone is sick and suffering. We don't have to drag around that luggage for the rest of our lives.

"We are too late for the past and too early for the future."

Have you ever thought to yourself that the only reality is this moment, right here, right now?

The past is gone. We cannot change it, so why not accept what once was? Forgive people and yourself, release any guilt and welcome yourself back into the present moment.

The future is not here yet and we have no way of telling what the future holds. So bring it back to the moment, trust and believe in God and start living life in the moment.

Once you arrive back in the moment tell yourself it is a safe place to be, hanging out with God.

"Some people are so poor, all they have is money."

Most people believe that money will buy happiness. Money can be nice, but not if you need it to fill the hole in your soul.

Some people use money to fuel their ego. They also use it to hide behind and to feel powerful.

Money also prevents us from trusting and believing in God. Instead of waiting for the magic and miracles to happen, money can make us use our own will and not let God show us the path.

Happiness is an inside job, and money is just a tool.

"When we look outward, we dream.
When we look inward, we awaken."

The longest journey is the journey inward. Few people will ever look at themselves to see the real person inside. The easier road is to point the finger and find blame with people, places, and things.

The spiritual warrior dares to look inward at themselves to find what they like and what they dislike. Then we have an opportunity to make a change from the things we don't like. This is the transformation you hear some people talking about. The change must start with you then you can begin to help others. That's when the magic and miracles will happen.

"Life is about wanting what you have,
not having what you want."

Gratitude is one of the most important tools for happiness. Until you awaken to the moment and find gratitude for all that you have, you will only find depression, wasting the moment thinking about what you don't have.

There can be no sustainable happiness found in the monetary and material world until you fill the hole in your soul with God.

No people, place, or thing will fill this void no matter how hard you try.

"Don't drive faster than your guardian angel can fly."

When we awaken to all the gifts we have received from modern technology we should not take for granted transportation. There are rules of the road for a reason because when there are no rules, anarchy rules. This is designed so we can arrive safe and not hurt other people.

Make a change today and be the awakened one who actually stops at the stop signs and red lights. Be the one who is not driving down the road speeding with their head down texting.

If you don't make that change, it's not "if" but "when" something bad is going to happen.

"The true meaning of success is measured in emotional balance, not check book balance."

*I*t seems that in the material world that if you are rich, it is okay to be a lunatic, but if you are poor and a lunatic you will have to go to a mental hospital.

Rich or poor we should be more focused on emotional balance to try to find the middle road. Notice if your life is upside down, or up and down like a yo-yo.

Begin to make the change. Respond to life's challenges in a positive way rather than react to life's challenges in a negative way. The health you will be saving is your own.

"Worrying is the same as paying interest on a loan that will never come due."

*W*orrying is one of the worst mind viruses that you can have. Worrying is fear, fear of the unknown and known, as well as fear of the past and of the future.

One tool you can use to combat worrying is faith. Faith is the opposite of fear. Fear knocked and faith answered.

Once we become aware of the fear in our life we can bring it back to the moment and ask God for help.

As we continue to practice the moment with God, positivity, and gratitude, you'll find there will be no need to worry unless you choose to ruin the moment yourself.

"There is no growth in the comfort zone."

As spiritual beings we must always welcome life's challenges and try to figure out the best way to feel, deal, and heal from these tests.

These tests are designed by God so we can grow spiritually. These tests, as you well know, do not always feel good to go through. These are the growing pains of the spiritual warriors. These challenges are going to keep coming whether you like it or not.

Why not change how we look at them and open ourselves to the opportunity of change?

"Be so busy with self-help, that you have no time to criticize others."

*I*t's super easy to criticize other people and what they are doing. Remember, if one finger is pointing out, there are three pointing back at you.

Instead, catch yourself in the moment that you are criticizing someone and turn it around to put a positive spin on it.

Reverse the curse and send that person positive energy and then pat yourself on the back for a job well done.

"Become willing to get better not bitter."

*A*ll people in this life have experienced hurt, pain, and loss. Hopefully we have also experienced happiness, love, and gain.

Unfortunately, people who have experienced hurt, pain, and loss, somehow can't seem to get over it and move on. It is very easy to get addicted to victimhood and take a dark outlook on the world and all people.

Once we become aware we can take action to reverse the curse of bitterness and seek help from professionals, support groups, and meditation.

Life is too long to drag around the pain of yesterday. So why not enjoy today.

"You can plan your future just don't plan your outcome."

As you may have noticed, one of the themes of this book is the moment. However, you may choose to use the moment to make plans for the future. This is all good as long as you don't leave the moment and start playing movies inside your head of what you think might happen with your plans of the future. When you leave the moment and start playing movies inside your head of the future you are missing out on the moment in which you are living.

After the plan is made stay grounded in the moment where God lives. There just might be a God story waiting for you.

"If you call yourself a perfectionist, and see all things as imperfect, than you are an imperfectionist."

We have all heard many people say that they are perfectionists, but they see most things as imperfect.

In life, there are few things that are perfect.

Instead, practice acceptance with the way that things are. All we can do is the best we can. After that, if we practice acceptance, we are less likely to drive ourselves crazy.

Just for today become willing to make a change to accept all things just as they are. You will be taking the weight of the world off your shoulders.

"Cooperation not competition."

When we invite competition into our lives we are inviting in a lot of stress and pressure that we don't really need or want.

Some people love to win, and when they don't it seems like the end of the world. No one can stay at the top forever.

The reason this way of life never works out is because of the ego calling all the shots.

Dare to team together with someone or a group of people with the same interest for the higher good.

You will be trading in stress and pressure for magic and miracles.

"Don't let people, places, and things blow your light out."

*O*nce we have awakened to the moment, God, positivity, and gratitude, a light will come on inside of you. This light will begin to shine especially through your eyes, the windows to your soul.

Asleep people with mind viruses (a.k.a. psychological terrorists), will try to blow your light out, with negativity and overall rudeness.

Try to have compassion for these people, for we were also once sick and suffering. Try not to take it personally. Remember hurt people hurt people. This is just what they do and you just happen to get caught in their cross hairs.

"We all have a free spirit it's just a matter
of allowing your spirit to be free."

*A*ll people wish to let their spirit be free and be a free spirit.

Getting drunk at the family barbecue and proclaiming your independence does not constitute you being free.

There will be no long term happiness found by signing contracts, loan papers, and credit card offers to achieve more materialism. What we are really doing is building our own self-made prison by becoming a slave to money and the job to try to make our ends meet.

While it is true that we all need food, clothing, and shelter, check in with yourself and see if you are the one with the bumper sticker that says "He who dies with the most toys wins".

You will never know what true freedom feels like until you stop financing your entire life, start working less, eating better, and getting a dog.

"When you wake up in the morning what will you do if all you have left is what you thanked God for yesterday?"

Once again, one of the most important tools for happiness is gratitude. We live in a world where so many people take things for granted and don't realize what they had until they lose someone or something.

Each day find things to be grateful for and watch your world change around you.

"Smooth seas don't make for skillful sailors."

Most people don't like problems or tough challenges. These tests are designed for our personal growth from the creator. Like it or not, life will sooner or later throw you a curve ball. It is your choice how you choose to respond to it. There is no personal growth in the comfort zone.

Instead, accept the challenge, ask for help, and try to see the bigger picture with spiritual eyes and positivity. Everything happens for a reason and hindsight is 20/20.

"Avoid low hanging fruit."

*L*ike it or not, we are who we hang out with. If we hang out with people who lie, steal, cheat, drink, and do drugs, we will end up absorbing much of their negative energy and will become like them. Remember, monkey see, monkey do, and monkey get in trouble too.

Instead, look for people with honesty, respect, and positivity. Don't take their word for it, all of these things will show in their actions. Listen to the words coming out of their mouth. Life changes when we become part of the solution not part of the problem.

"Think before you speak, ask yourself, 'are the words that are about to come out of my mouth, going to help or hurt someone?'"

Once we have arrived in the moment, we all have choices, positive or negative.

Remember Grandma taught us to think before we speak? That is because Grandma knew about the wisdom, magic, and miracles.

Practice saying something positive or kind instead of saying something hurtful, negative, prejudice, or sarcastic.

"If you don't lie, you don't have to remember."

*T*elling lies is a full time job. You always have to be remembering the lies you tell people.

It's much easier to tell the truth because you won't have to remember who you lied to.

It makes life much easier and makes way for peace and serenity in the moment.

"God gave us two hands for a reason,
one for giving and one for receiving."

*A*ll people want balance in their life whether they know it or not. This is why God gave us two hands, one for giving and one for receiving.

Notice if you only give and don't feel good when you receive. Identify why it makes you feel this way and reverse the curse today.

Also, notice if you only receive and don't feel good when you give. Once again, identify why you feel this way and make the change today. Once we become in balance we will be getting right with the moment.

"We all have personal baggage. The key is finding the right baggage handler."

All people come with emotional and personal baggage from the past. The key to a successful relationship is to find the right person to enjoy life with.

We need to be tolerant and compassionate towards other people's baggage as they need to be for our luggage.

Nobody is perfect and neither are we.

"As children, we believed in magic, that anything is possible. The trick is to never stop believing in magic."

When we first came to this planet, we were happy, in the moment, curious, and fearless. Then through a series of events our magic got taken away (usually by our parents).

The key is to become aware of this and work on getting our childlike wonder, magic, and miracles back.

"Feel, deal, and heal."

This is the process in how we should handle all of life's problems. When unfortunate circumstances happen in our lives that cause pain, most people head for an addiction to temporarily help them feel better. This includes alcohol, drugs, sex, food, work, or retail therapy. This will only lead to more pain and suffering. Remember, pain is inevitable but suffering is optional.

Only by feeling the feelings and experiencing the experiences can you then learn to deal and ultimately heal.

"You spend most of your adulthood
getting over your childhood."

*I*f you think about your childhood and are honest about it, most of us suffered some traumas, dramas, issues, and tissues.

Become aware of this and get involved with some kind of self-help or support group. By doing this you'll be getting the help you need and begin to feel, deal, and heal.

*"Say what you mean, mean what you say,
but don't be mean when you say it."*

*I*t is important to tell people if you feel they did or said something to harm you.

The important thing is to tell them in a kind way, just like you would want done to you if you had said or done something to hurt somebody.

"People very rarely fail, they simply stop trying."

Sometimes on the path of life we will hit a road block and feel like giving up.

This is the time to warrior up. Ask God and people for help. Why not try thinking in different ways to achieve your goals? Most great people had to jump many high hurdles to get where they are today.

"Hurt people, hurt people."

Most people are victims of some kind of abuse in one form or another. This is why they continue the vicious cycle of abuse.

Once we awaken to the fact that we hurt people because we ourselves got hurt, that's when the healing can begin.

Healing will start once we stop hurting people including ourselves. Become aware of this today and stop this epidemic by practicing kindness.

"Honesty without compassion is brutality."

*O*nce we change from being generally or compulsively dishonest to honest, we'll have the tendency to become brutally honest because we have not yet developed our spiritual filtration system.

This is where working with a spiritual advisor can help. Before reacting to a situation it is wise to pause and seek spiritual guidance to be able to tell someone the truth without hurting them. This is called responding versus reacting.

Once you begin to see how this works the universe will reflect its light back at you. What you have created is a better world for you to live in.

"If you wish for a million dollars,
you wish for a million problems."

*I*f you think about it, money is only green paper with dead presidents on it. While it is true that money is needed to survive these days, it does not have to become our only way of life.

Many people who have won the lottery will tell a story of how they wish they never got that money to begin with. Let's learn from their mistakes.

If you have enough money for today, along with food, clothing, and shelter, you have everything you need to find happiness.

"Nature doesn't lie, so look to nature."

Nature is the essence of true magic. The ways of nature are undisputed truths. It works perfectly in balance until man gets in the way. Man has unlocked some of nature's magic, but there is still a lot we don't know.

Nature has no hidden agendas. Respect nature by asking before taking and being grateful for what has been received. Nature has its own laws for us to connect and live in harmony with her, the earth mother. She has compassion for the way man has been mistreating her, so let's awaken and be kind to her today.

"A grateful heart and mind never complains."

nce again, gratitude should be at the forefront of our moment. No happiness can be achieved by complaining. It is impossible to be in the moment with gratitude and be complaining at the same time.

Complaining is actually you criticizing God's plan. If it is raining out today and you get wet, try not to complain. We need this water to drink and water our crops and trees. Without water life will cease to exist. Try to think of these things in a spiritual way and less about yourself. You will begin to see life in a different light.

*"**Less** is more."*

*I*n the material and monetary world we are taught to believe the more we have, the more happiness can be achieved. In America, we have the most abundance, and yet we have the most people on anti-depressants or some other mind altering drug, legal or illegal.

The truth is that happiness cannot be found in money, materialism, or a pill. It can be found in God, the moment, humility, gratitude, positivity, and love.

Some of the most grounded, spiritual people will tell you that when they gave up all their big ticket items and started to simplify their lives, the weight of the world came off their shoulders and they found happiness and freedom.

"Don't get taken hostage by mentally ill, psychological terrorist."

elfish, mentally ill people love to find others to take hostage and do all the talking about the negativity in the world.

It is nice to lend an ear to listen to people and what they have to say. However, if it is not a two way conversation and they are unwilling to listen, it is difficult to help them. It's okay to excuse yourself. They will have no problem finding a new victim.

"A problem shared is a problem cut in half."

When we live inside our own heads with life's challenges, problems, and secrets we are actually creating more problems for ourselves. When we are caught in the emotion we are not mentally clear enough to make the right decision for ourselves.

When we reach out to another person we trust we will get the right answers we need to get us through.

"If you want to make God laugh, tell God your plans."

When we make plans for the future with rigidity we are all setting ourselves up for a good laugh.

This is not how the universe operates. God does not live in the future, God lives in the now, so how could we know what the future is going to hold for us?

Once again, the most important thing is to stay grounded in the moment, working on ourselves to be the best person we can be, here and now.

"What other people think of you is none of your business."

A lot of people worry about what people think of them. This has two negatives built within it.

First, what a waste of a moment it is worrying about someone or something. We are all in God's hands.

Remember, faith is the opposite of fear and worrying is fear out of control.

Second, we have no control over people, places or things, although our egos will tell us something different. Most people are plagued with mind viruses, so why be concerned with what someone thinks of you when their thoughts are contaminated with negativities?

"When the student is ready, the teacher appears."

We have to travel down all the roads until we get to the moment in which we awaken. It usually comes in the form of a teacher. Remember God works through people and animals too.

You will undoubtedly know when this is happening because the universe will begin to make a little more sense. Then you will have a thirst for self-help, wisdom, magic, and miracles. You will start to understand what is really important and stop complaining and sweating the small stuff. The teacher appears when God knows you are ready to receive the messages.

"A bad attitude is like a flat tire,
until you fix it you won't get very far."

Check in with yourself today. What kind of attitude toward life do you have? Do you have an attitude of gratitude?

A positive attitude is an essential part of each moment of each day. Without it you are in alignment with darkness and negativity.

Once again, reverse the curse and put a positive spin on your attitude today. You won't understand how much magic this holds until you try it yourself.

"We row, God steers."

Self-help and spirituality are action words. It is difficult to do self- help work in front of the TV with a half gallon of ice cream. We will not find any God stories watching reruns of your favorite TV shows.

We have to put forth the effort and energy to transform our lives here on earth.

Once on the right track, you can strive for positive goals such as peace of mind, serenity, truth, and happiness. You can rest assured God will steer you in the right direction.

"Some people say, 'when things change, that's when I will be happy, but when I choose to be happy, that's when things will change.'"

*I*t is an illusion to believe that happiness is achieved when you find that so called right person, job promotion, top of the line automobile, or the home of your dreams.

Different circumstances in the future may bring you short term happiness, only to be followed by unhappiness.

What you will actually be doing is continuing to put yourself on the emotional rollercoaster ride when you try to seek happiness outside of yourself.

Why not choose to find happiness here and now. By doing this you will be guaranteed to find happiness in the future. Be grateful for the things you have today, and not depressed for the things you have not.

Choose happiness in each moment of each day, regardless of what's happening around you. Remember, God will never give you more than you can handle.

Made in the USA
Middletown, DE
12 September 2022

72747362R00055